A Circle of Friends

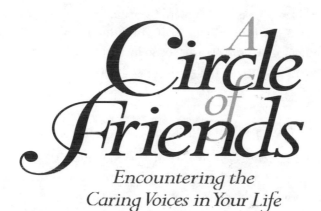

A Circle of Friends

Encountering the Caring Voices in Your Life

Robert J. Wicks
Robert M. Hamma

AVE MARIA PRESS
Notre Dame, Indiana 46556

First printing, January, 1996
Second printing, July, 1998
16,000 copies in print

International Standard Book Number: 0-87793-574-2

Library of Congress Catalog Card Number: 95-83179

Cover design by Elizabeth French

Printed and bound in the United States of America.

Contents

*I*ntroduction

*T*his book began as a dinner conversation. In the almost ten years that I have been Bob Wicks's editor, our relationship has grown and changed. What began as a professional relationship has become a friendship. This has happened despite the fact that we see one another infrequently. That, of course, makes the opportunities for face-to-face conversation all the more valuable.

It was at one such meeting that Bob proposed to me the idea of taking the chapter on friends from his book *Touching the Holy* and publishing it as a little book of its own. I remember him commenting on what a positive response he has received to that material at his many talks and retreats. This was one of my favorite chapters in the book too, so I was enthused about the idea.

The first time I read the chapter I thought about all the different people who had gifted me with their friendship in the different modes that Bob described: prophet, cheerleader, harasser, and spiritual guide. I proposed to Bob that this new book should help people explore further how they perform these roles in their relationships as well as help them reflect on their openness to hearing these voices from others. "Perhaps you could come up with characteristics for each of these roles, something to help people identify behaviors that are part of each type of friend," I suggested. "Maybe you could create exercises to help readers grow more comfortable in these roles and to become more receptive to these voices."

Bob gave me a look of disbelief. "Where did all that come from?" he asked.

"I don't know, I just think that's a terrific chapter and you could do a lot with it."

We went away from our dinner agreeing to think about it. A week later Bob called. "Listen," he said, "I think we should do that book together. You have a lot of thought-provoking ideas, and we could spell them out together." Regardless of your definition of friendship, trust plays a big part in it. In the years we've worked together, I've learned to trust him and he has been willing to trust me with his manuscripts. I know that I can take a free hand with his work and do my best as

an editor to make it better. He is always receptive and grateful.

This little book is the result of our mutual trust
and friendship. Since both of us like to write in
the first person at times, we decided to each
share our personal experiences in that voice. So
be aware that when you read "I" it may be one
or the other of us speaking to you. The brief
biographies at the end of the book will provide
some help identifying who the speaker is.

◆ *Bob Hamma*

ONE

Friends for the Journey

You are my intimate friend. . . .

I will make all my beauty pass before you,

and in your presence I will pronounce my name.

◆ *Exodus 33: 17-19*

Friendship has been by far the chief source of my happiness.

◆ *C. S. Lewis*

*O*ne of the best definitions of friendship I have found comes from the Scottish philosopher John Macmurray: "To be a friend is to be yourself for another person."

Friendship begins with being yourself. It cannot be programmed; it cannot be forced. As the fox in the *Little Prince* said, "[There is] no shop anywhere where one can buy friendship." Friendship is a gift, offered from one person to another.

When my son was in first grade, one of his biggest concerns was having a best friend. He had had many friends in his preschool and kindergarten. But now he was in a totally new environment, a much larger school with many more students. I knew that it was just a matter of time till he would forge new friendships. But from his viewpoint, the issue was much greater. The question he was asking himself was, "Will anyone like me?" The only thing I could think to tell him was this: "If you want to have a friend, you first have to be a friend."

Am I Lovable?

All of us have stood in that fearful and uncertain place from time to time, wondering if we are really likable, lovable. And we have learned that friendship can only happen when we have the courage simply to be ourselves. Where does that courage come from? It comes from the experience of being loved. When someone has loved the real me, the person behind the exterior facade, my hidden true self, then I have the courage to love in return.

That kind of unconditional love is what we're supposed to get from our parents. As I watched my son go off to the uncertainties of first grade, I could only hope that the love we had given him would be enough to sustain him. But many of us have not gotten the unconditional love in childhood that we need to ground a healthy sense of self. We have a hard time believing that anyone will like us.

The *Saturday Night Live* character Stuart Smalley offers a pitiful caricature of this situation with his mantra, "I'm good enough, I'm smart enough, and gosh darn it, people like me." But as we all know, just saying it doesn't make it so. To get to the point of believing we are lovable is often a process of unlearning the negative messages we have received about ourselves and relearning that we are made in the image of a loving God.

Unlearning is a process of identifying the negative messages we have received and absorbed into our psyches and replacing them with a realistic, healthy sense of self. In each of our personal histories, we have inevitably received a fair number of negative messages from others. Even the best of parents or significant adults can, often without knowing it, project their own needs and demands onto us. As a result, their love was not always unconditional. Our inability to live up to these expectations is one of the basic building blocks of a negative self-image.

To make matters more complicated, as children we also took into ourselves unconsciously some of the self-esteem deficits that the significant adults in our lives might have had at the time. Because they were our guides, we followed them without question. We patterned our behavior on theirs in ways that were rarely spoken about. What they subtly modeled, we quickly learned.

In addition to the negative messages and styles of acting that we received from adults during our formative years, there were the many hurtful, sometimes cruel things said and done to us by our peers.

I recall, for example, the relentless and unmerciful way that the Cub Scouts in my pack would tease a certain boy they said had body odor, chanting "B.O. Breslin . . . B.O. Breslin." While I was at times subjected to a similar type of teasing because I wore thick glasses, it was the fear of such ridicule as much as the actual mockery itself that motivated me to try at all costs to fit in with the group.

Each of us carries around similar memories of childhood. Whether we were the victims of this kind of teasing or perhaps at times the perpetrators of it, the need to fit in and the sense that we have to prove ourselves to be accepted can become paralyzing obstacles to growth in friendship.

Because we have often picked up such negative messages and patterns of behavior without even knowing it, it can be very difficult to identify them. Our reactions to a negative message now can give us a clue to the latent power of these messages in the past. It is not unusual to hear people say: "I know I am a good person. I know I have many talents and people respect me. But when I do something wrong or someone says something negative about me, it seems to undo all the positives. I believe the single negative comment rather than all the positive ones. I think it expresses how people really feel about me and what, deep down, I really believe about myself."

This type of response is an indication that there is some unlearning to be done. Informal forms of self reflection; feedback from friends, family, and colleagues; and structured interactions with therapists, counselors, or spiritual guides are helpful ways of checking the accuracy of our self-image.

In addition, "Principles of Self Respect and Clarity," "Imagery Exercises," and the technique of "heartstorming" outlined in *Touching the Holy* will be helpful.

But growth toward the sense of security that enables us "to be ourselves for another person" also requires relearning. Perhaps the most fundamental relearning that each of us must do—over and over—is to accept that we are made in the image and likeness of God. Genesis affirms the goodness of all creation and human beings as the crown of God's handiwork: "God saw everything that he had made, and indeed, it was very good" (1:31). The author of Ephesians also reminds us that we are made in God's image with these words: "We are God's work of art" (Eph 2:10). And the early church writer St. Irenaeus said: "The glory of God is a human being who is fully alive."

In his wonderful book, *Friendship in the Lord,* Paul Hinnebusch writes: "God does not love us because we are good. We are good because God loves us. His love makes us good by drawing to full development the potentialities which he himself has lovingly created in us. Each one of us is a wonderful mystery of his love."

As a parent I often marvel at the unexpected gifts that my children possess. My five-year-old daughter, for example, loves coloring and painting and is quite interested in art. One of her favorite places is the local art museum. Neither my wife nor I have much talent in this area, so it is a surprising joy to see her interest and ability.

Her gift is a reflection of a potential that God lovingly created in her, a prism on the wonderful mystery of God's love. If only we could see our own gifts with the same relish and joy that loving parents have when they behold the unique abilities of each of their children. Instead, rather than accepting our gifts gratefully, we tend to compare them negatively to those of others.

To take to heart the beautiful words that we are made in God's image, we need the experience of being loved. It is only when we experience for ourselves the presence of Jesus saying to us, "You are my friend" (Jn 15:14), that we can begin to build friendships based on his call to "love one another . . . just as I have loved you" (Jn 13:34).

To Be a Friend

Not only is each of us created in God's image, each of us is a unique reflection of God. We seem to have little trouble believing the fact that each snowflake is unique, but when it comes to believing that about ourselves, it is quite a different story.

Accepting our uniqueness means that we each have something to offer in a friendship that only we can give. Philip Mooney reflects in *Belonging Always* on Macmurray's definition of friendship:

> *I*t is the spirit of care that is unique in each of us. . . . Your spirit of care comes forth from your uniqueness appreciating the unique worth of the other, and it brims over in your gift of yourself to that person. And when that other person, warmed by the touch of your concern, responds in his or her characteristic way of expressing care, friendship begins to knit.

Our particular "spirit of care" is the gift we have to bring to a friendship. It is our "true face." It is the name by which God calls us. To be a friend, as Mooney points out, is to take the risk of offering that gift of self, in our uniqueness, to another.

When that gift is accepted, a sense of appreciation bursts forth. Acceptance by another fulfills our heart's longing and increases our ability to appreciate ourselves. Hinnebusch writes: "The deepest desire of our being is to be known, because only in being fully known and lovingly appreciated can we fully be. The whole thrust of our being is to be appreciated."

There is more to a friendship, of course, than simply appreciating each other's uniqueness. Although the early stages of a friendship are often characterized by an exciting sense of mutual discovery, the real substance of a friendship is in the actual caring for another. While the courage to extend the gift of friendship often requires a great deal of self-consciousness on our part, the *growth* of the friendship will require a corresponding forgetfulness of ourselves.

There are many virtues necessary to be a good friend. As we look at the various models of friendship in the subsequent chapters, we will explore some of them more deeply. For now, there are three that I would like to highlight: presence, patience, and perseverance. They are necessary regardless of what direction a relationship takes.

Presence

For anything to happen in a relationship, we have to be present to one another. "A friend is someone who is there for me, somebody I can count on," we often say. Friends like to be together; they make sacrifices to be together. In times of trouble they make it a priority to be together. Ideally, we can be present in person. But even if circumstances keep friends apart, they will find ways to be present to one another by phone, by letter, or, more likely in today's world, by E-mail.

The quality of our time with friends is important. The opportunity for good conversation, recreation, or participation together in some project is essential. But in our quest for quality time, we sometimes overlook the value of "non-quality" time. One of the richest dimensions of long friendships is the fact that such friends have seen each other at their worst. They know one another's failings, they recognize each other's negative patterns of behavior, and they know one another's fears. But they still care deeply for one another.

Patience

In any relationship there are three aspects: each of the two individuals and also the relationship they share together. Patience applies to all three. First, we must be patient with ourselves—with our insecurities, neediness, and limitations. And we must be patient with the inclination or even the need to try to be all things for our friends. Friendships can sometimes fail because we forget that what we are bringing to another is our special capacity to care for that person. We can only be what we are, a unique person with a special ability to care.

The word *patience* comes from a Latin word meaning "to suffer." Patience toward our friends requires that we be willing to suffer *through* as well as to suffer *with*. Just as we are limited, so are our friends. The difficulty is that their limitations are often different from ours, and thus we find it hard to understand them. Because a particular issue may not be a source of anxiety for us, we may find ourselves saying, "I don't understand why this is such a problem for you."

For example, I find it relatively easy to ask others about themselves. I can keep a person talking about himself or herself for quite a while. But it is harder for me to initiate a conversation focused on me. I tend to expect my friends to do for me what I do for them; that is, I expect them to ask me all sorts of interesting questions about my work, whatever book I'm reading, my garden, and so on. When my friends don't do this, I get a little resentful; it seems as though they don't care. But in fact, it's a case of my abilities being different from theirs. I need to learn to be patient with myself and with them. This involves learning to see things through our friends' eyes.

Perseverance

The third aspect of a friendship is the relationship we share. Paul Hinnebusch describes a friendship as "two people growing." We grow separately, and we grow together. A relationship has stages that cannot be rushed or forced. There will be times of closeness and times of distance. There will be hurts that need forgiveness. Without perseverance a friendship will not last.

A friendship cannot be molded according to preexisting expectations. Each friendship is different. One person cannot be made to resemble another. Nor can we seek to replace the unique qualities of a lost or distant relationship with those of a new one. Only with perseverance will we discover the uniqueness of each relationship.

To Be a Spiritual Friend

A spiritual friend is someone who shares our spiritual journey. All friends do that for one another, often unknowingly. But here I am talking about a relationship in which we are comfortable in making this spiritual dimension explicit. We should be careful not to define the term spiritual too narrowly. It obviously includes such things as prayer and faith, but it is much more than that.

A spiritual friend is someone with whom we can celebrate God's presence and action in our lives. There is a freedom in the relationship to talk about what we hear God saying to us, how we discovered God anew, or where we feel God is present in our lives at this moment.

A spiritual friend helps us explore and express our sense of vocation. Whether we are married, in religious life, in the priesthood, or single, a spiritual companion is someone with whom we can discuss the motivations that keep us going in life, someone who helps us remember why we are doing what we do.

An important role of a spiritual friend is to help us gain perspective. In *Exploring Spiritual Direction* Alan Jones writes:

> [*A* friend is someone who gives us] a new perspective. He or she is able to stir up our imagination so that we not only view the past differently, but also allow the future to be pregnant with new and exciting possibilities. . . . Sometimes all it takes to bring about the miracle of new hope is a tiny shift in perspective, like a painter seeing a whole new landscape merely by changing the position of the easel.

A spiritual friend is someone who helps us in the large and small decisions we must make. Such a friend helps us sift through our experience to weigh the reasons for and against a decision. He or she helps us attend to our feelings about the alternatives before us. And a spiritual friend helps us recognize where the Spirit of God is most present to us.

A spiritual friend helps us say yes to the call to empty ourselves, to accept the cross; helps us identify when we are truly being called to let go, to die a little. And a spiritual friend knows us well enough to blow the whistle when we are simply giving in to a pattern of self-destructive behavior that has no potential to be life-giving.

In *Mentor and Friend* Timothy K. Jones suggests three "reasonable hopes" for a relationship with a spiritual friend:

1. Expect to find immense support simply from another's presence.

2. Expect a spiritual guide to help make new sense of everyday life.

3. Expect a guide to help ground the spiritual life in something more solid than private experience or personal opinion.

These three expectations can also be read as characteristics of a sound spiritual friendship. A spiritual friend supports us, helps us make sense of our lives, and grounds us in reality. Such a friend is, indeed, a companion for the journey.

The Voice of Jesus, Your Friend

Reflect on this passage in which Jesus speaks prophetically to a friend:

The next day John again was standing with two of his disciples, and as he watched Jesus walk by he exclaimed, "Look, here is the Lamb of God!" The two disciples heard him say this, and they followed Jesus. When Jesus turned and saw them following, he said to them, "What are you looking for?" They said to him, "Rabbi" (which translated means Teacher), "where are you staying?" He said to them, "Come and see" (Jn 1:35-39).

Friendships sometimes begin naturally, sometimes unexpectedly. When the two disciples in this passage responded to Jesus' invitation to come and see where he lived, they probably had no sense that this was the beginning of a friendship that would change their lives.

◆ Place yourself in this episode. With the disciples, ask, "Teacher, where do you live?" How does Jesus respond to you?

◆ Reflect on a significant relationship in your life. How did it begin? What invitation did you give to the other to enter into your life? What invitation did you receive?

◆ Focus on a particular time when you realized that Jesus was a friend. How did the invitation to that friendship come into your life? What was your response?

Recognizing the Friends in Your Life

◆ With whom do you feel free simply to be yourself?

◆ What qualities do you value most highly in a friend?

◆ As you reflect on your friends, are there any qualities that they share in common? What are the special qualities of each person?

◆ Complete the following sentences:

Someone whose simple presence offers me immense support is . . .

Someone who helps me make new sense of everyday life is . . .

Someone who helps me ground my spiritual life in something more solid than my private experience or personal opinion is . .

Being a Friend

◆ What in your life is an obstacle to your being a better friend? Is there anything you need to unlearn?

◆ What is the particular spirit of care that you bring to a friendship?

◆ In what ways do you bring the gifts of presence, patience, and perseverance to the relationships in your lives?

Journal Exercises

◆ What is your personal definition of friendship?

◆ Make a time line of your life, noting on it the most significant moments. Write the name of the person or persons who were closest to you at each of those times. What role did they play?

TWO

Types of Friends

A faithful friend is a sturdy shelter,

A faithful friend is beyond price,

A faithful friend is a life-saving remedy.

◆ *Sirach 6: 14-1*(NAB)

There is no problem in collecting from many different flowers the honey which we cannot find in one flower only.

◆ *Francis de Sales*

*T*here is a wonderful story in the second chapter of Mark's gospel in which Jesus heals a paralytic. Jesus has just returned to Capernaum after a tour around the villages of Galilee in which he preached, healed the sick, and expelled demons. He is once again preaching "in front of the door" of what seems to be Simon's house, the same place where he had recently cured Simon's mother-in-law.

A huge crowd has assembled to hear him. "So many had gathered around that there was no longer room for them," the gospel tells us. Some people were trying to bring a paralyzed man to Jesus, but they could not make their way through the crowd. So they went around to the back of the house and carried him up to the roof, using the outside stairway typical of Palestinian houses.

The man was carried by "four of them" (Mk 2:3). Four people would have been needed to carry the stretcher, particularly up the stairs.

Some commentators think that these four may have been Simon, Andrew, James, and John. To this point in Mark's story, these are the only four disciples who have been called, and the four of them were named as having stayed at Simon's house on the first visit to Capernaum. One can easily imagine these four cooking up a scheme that would provide Jesus with a chance to demonstrate his healing power, particularly in front of the local scribes who were part of the attentive crowd. And knowing what we do about Simon Peter, it is hard to imagine that he would have let anyone else start pulling apart the roof of his house!

That is what these four did: Ripping off the thatched roof and the supporting beams, they lower the man down to the floor. Jesus notices their faith, but rather than healing the man's physical ills, he says, "Son, your sins are forgiven you." This remark touches off the first of many confrontations between Jesus and the scribes related in Mark's gospel. The story reaches its climax when Jesus demonstrates his authority to forgive sins by healing the paralyzed man.

This is a rich episode, full of important themes for understanding Mark's gospel, as well as for prayerful reflection. But for our purpose here, I'd like to focus on a detail that might otherwise be lost—the role of the four stretcher-bearers. If in fact these were Simon, Andrew, James, and John, we can imagine that Simon and Andrew would have known the paralyzed man, being residents of the same small village. They may even have been his friends.

But regardless of whether we can know their identities, these four people certainly acted as friends to the paralytic. Without them, he would not have been able to get to Jesus and he would not have been healed. We can imagine that they had the idea to bring him to Jesus, that they went and got him, that they persuaded him to come along, and that they actually carried him there. It was their faith (not the faith of the paralytic alone, as Mark's gospel notes), that prompted Jesus' response.

As we enter into this exploration of the role of friendship in our spiritual journeys, this story can provide a keynote for considering the types of friends we need. In subsequent chapters we will focus on four types of friends: *prophet, cheerleader, harasser,* and *spiritual guide*. But for now, let's engage in a symbolic interpretation of this passage and imagine that each of these four stretcher-bearers represents one of these types of friends.

The prophet is a person who challenges us to take a good look at ourselves, to re-evaluate some attitude or action. The cheerleader is a person who offers us enthusiastic, unconditional acceptance. The cheerleader comforts us, encourages us, and offers us unwavering faith and support. The harasser helps us to change our perspective when we are taking ourselves too seriously. With gentle humor the harasser keeps us from getting too caught up in ourselves. The spiritual guide is the friend who helps us recognize our unique gifts and discern the directions before us.

In order for the paralytic to get to Jesus, he needed the help of his friends. Perhaps he needed a prophet to point out to him that God was truly working through this Jesus and that he needed to listen to him. He may have needed a cheerleader to encourage him that there was something to hope for here. Perhaps he was more than a little resistant, down on himself and wallowing in his misery. In that case he would have needed a harasser to stop him from taking his pain so seriously and to look at things from a different perspective. Certainly he would have needed a spiritual guide to help him recognize his heart's deepest longing and to find the faith to say yes to it.

In the gospel there were four who bore his litter. While this may have been the most practical way to do it, it certainly wasn't the only way. Three could have done it, or perhaps two. Even one friend, if strong enough, could have picked the man up and carried him.

Just so for us too. While it might be ideal to have one or more people who can perform each of these roles for us, that is not always possible. While we often refer to them as types, we should also think of them as "voices." At different times the same person may speak with two or more of these voices. It is not that we have to have four friends, each with a gift for one of these roles. We need a friend who knows us well enough to speak in the voice we need to hear when we need to hear it.

As we reflect on our own experience of giving and receiving the gift of friendship, we may discover that there is a particular role that suits us best. This is, to use Philip Mooney's phrase, our unique "spirit of care." While this may be our natural voice, we can speak in other voices as well, though perhaps not as easily.

What is true of us is likely to be true of our friends as well. The more we can be open to cultivating many friendships and receiving the special gift of care from others, the more likely we are to have the variety of voices we need in our lives.

Henri Nouwen, in *Making All Things New*, writes: "We can take a lot of physical and even mental pain when we know that it truly makes us a part of the life we live together in the world. But when we feel cut off from the human family, we quickly lose heart." Like the paralytic in Mark's gospel, we've all experienced times when our pain has made us feel cut off from the world. Hopefully, like him, we have discovered that friendship, in a very real sense, is a vital link not only to a small intimate circle of trusted others, but the connecting point that opens us out to a larger world, to the whole human family. The work I have done with persons experiencing emotional stress, spiritual hunger, and personal alienation has taught me that if we don't trust others to help us along the way, a debilitating sense of isolation can sometimes take over.

Many of us face the practical problem that our friends are often unavailable to us. The ready-made community that we discovered in early adulthood—in college, at church, at work, through our children, in religious formation, or in the seminary—may still play a role in our lives. But as the demands of our particular vocation and the needs of those who depend on us take center stage, our friends may become less and less available, and new situations may bring new friends.

On the one hand, the demands of others may limit our time. On the other, what we can accomplish as individuals seems to become more important to us. At the very time we need friends to offer balance, support, and perspective in our lives, our community of friends becomes less present to us. This is a shame, because friends are not only important for support, but they are also necessary for psychological and spiritual growth—and for holiness.

That is why books, lectures, and counselors stress the need to see a special value in establishing, maintaining, and further developing a more balanced community of friends. Trying to mature psychologically through sheer effort or to grow spiritually through individualistic forms of piety tends to spell disaster.

Recognition of the fact that friends are necessary not just to avoid the loneliness of isolation, but to encourage us to greater personal depth and openness is a first step. But we still face the practical and difficult task of nurturing relationships that can provide the challenge and support we need to grow.

Friends are not always easy to find. One study showed that as many as seventy percent of Americans said they had many acquaintances but few close friends. Even in the best of social times, the number of friends we have varies. That is, of course, natural. But if we reflect on what helps us grow, I think we will discover that while the presence of friends is essential, the variety and mix of friends in our lives can be almost equally important. Without a variety of voices in our community, we run the risk that our experiences and perceptions will be too limited, and that this will be reflected in our emotional and spiritual life.

When we try to live a committed life without a rich community, negative feelings can result. We can be paralyzed by feelings such as boredom, apathy, loneliness, burnout, self-righteousness, anger, restlessness, depression, moodiness, ambivalence, and anxiety. Even though such emotions usually have social, financial, physical, and psychological causes, they often have a spiritual side as well. As a matter of fact, although the cause and symptoms may vary, the primary source of such negative feelings may well be spiritual in nature.

A rich mixture of friends can help us improve our sense of psychological perspective and can further engender spiritual single-heartedness. Whether we find ourselves in painful or joyful circumstances, in the midst of confusion or relaxed in a comfortable period, friends can reach out to us. Whether by helping us find the way when we are temporarily lost or by rejoicing in the present moment, they can help us open new opportunities to meet God in surprising ways.

There is a hidden beauty in the thicket of ordinariness. That beauty is revealed, supported, and enhanced by the presence of good friends. But ordinary life also brings pain, difficulty, and sometimes tragedy. With the support of friends, life is not only bearable, it can be hope-filled.

Friends Who Carry *Us to* Jesus

Reflect on the following passage in light of the comments in this chapter:

When he returned to Capernaum after some days, it was reported that he was at home. So many gathered around that there was no longer room for them, not even in front of the door; and he was speaking the word to them. Then some people came, bringing to him a paralyzed man, carried by four of them. And when they could not bring him to Jesus because of the crowd, they removed the roof above him; and after having dug through it, they let down the mat on which the paralytic lay. When Jesus saw their faith he said to the paralytic, "Son, your sins are forgiven." Now some of the scribes were sitting there, questioning in their hearts, "Why does this fellow speak in this way? It is blasphemy! Who can forgive sins but God alone?" At once Jesus perceived in his spirit that they were discussing these questions among themselves; and he said to them, "Why do you raise such questions in your hearts? Which is easier, to say to the paralytic, 'Your sins are forgiven,' or to say, 'Stand up and walk'? But so that you may know that the Son of Man has authority on earth to forgive sins"—he said to the paralytic, "I say to you, stand up, take your mat and go to your home." And he stood up, and immediately took the mat and went out before all of them; so that they were all amazed and glorified God, saying, "We have never seen anything like this!" (Mk 2:1-12).

◆ In what relationships do you act like the friends who carried the paralytic to Jesus? How in your life are you like the paralytic?

◆ "When Jesus saw their faith he said to the paralytic, 'Son, your sins are forgiven.'" Who are the people whose faith is a supportive and healing presence to you?

Recognizing the Friends in Your Life

◆ Who is your oldest friend? How has that relationship evolved over the years?

◆ What qualities do you value most highly in a friend?

◆ At this point in your life, are you satisfied

with the availability of your friends to you? If not, what would you like to do about that?

◆ How open are you to cultivating new friendships at this time?

◆ What dangers does isolation present for you?

Being a Friend

◆ Who considers you a good friend? How do you attempt to offer your presence and support to that friend?

◆ What inhibits you from reaching out to others in friendship? What is one step you can take to correct this inhibition?

◆ In what ways do you bring the gifts of presence, patience, and perseverance to your relationships with others?

Journal Exercise

*I*magine yourself as the paralytic in this story—either in the actual situation described in the gospel or in a personal circumstance in which you are experiencing some form of physical, emotional, or spiritual paralysis. Who are the four people carrying your stretcher to Jesus? List their names and write what you would say to each one of them.

THREE

The Prophet

O that today you would listen to
God's voice!

Do not harden your hearts.

◆ *Psalm 95: 7-8*

A soul which is left alone
is like a burning coal left by itself:
It will grow colder rather than
hotter.

◆ *John of the Cross*

*T*he first of these roles or voices that help us maintain balance and have a sense of openness is the one I shall refer to as the prophet. Contrary to what one might imagine, prophetic friends need not look or behave any differently than other types of persons who are close to us. In reality, prophets only occasionally present themselves like John the Baptist: wild, woolly, and obvious. Often people who do come across that way are not really prophets at all.

A real prophet is a person who does not merely talk about truth but is an actual bearer and living model of the truth. John L. McKenzie writes: "The concept of Old Testament prophecy is that God spoke *through* the prophets or *in* the prophets. . . . It is to be noticed that God speaks *through* the prophets rather than *to* them." The Hebrew scriptures offer us quite a variety of types when it comes to prophets—the forceful Amos, the compassionate Hosea, the visionary Ezekiel, and the poetic Isaiah, among others. We likewise find variety in how the prophets communicated. Prophetic activity was not limited to words only. The prophets often performed symbolic actions as well, such as smashing a clay pot or even going naked through the city!

When it comes to the prophetic voice in our friendships, we may often find that the true prophets are not those who set out to be prophetic. It may well be that our friends speak prophetically to us without intending to or even realizing it. If there was one quality the various prophets shared, it was their initial reluctance to respond to God. So we might well be wary of those who are overly enthusiastic about prophesying to us, especially those who claim to have received a word for us!

The true prophet's voice is often quiet and fleeting but nonetheless strong. Prophets live honest, courageous lives guided by truth and compassion. With the grace of God they try to live out the truth, and, whether knowingly or not, they follow the advice of Gandhi: "Let our first act every morning be this resolve: I shall not fear anyone on earth. I shall fear only God. I shall not bear ill-will toward anyone. I shall conquer untruth by truth, and in resisting untruth, I shall put up with all suffering."

False prophets often come across in a convincingly dramatic way. I do not doubt that they have had a special encounter with God at one or more points in their lives. But somewhere along the way they have made a crucial error, one from which we can all learn. They have forgotten the place of grace in their own lives and are consequently taking themselves, instead of God, very seriously. Due to this, their personalities are projecting themselves so loudly that they can no longer hear the quiet, prophetic voice that should be guiding their own behavior. Thus they are in no position to help others in need.

The messages of prophets often involve discomfort or pain, though they are not the cause of the conflict. However, like leaders in the nonviolent movement, they may call it up, as is pointed out in the following words of Martin Luther King, Jr.:

> We who engage in nonviolent, direct action are not the creators of tension. We merely bring to the surface the hidden tension that is already alive. We bring it out in the open, where it can be seen and dealt with. Like a boil that can never be cured so long as it is covered up but must be opened with all its ugli-

ness to the natural medicines of air and
light, injustice must be exposed, with all
the tension its exposure creates, to the
light of human conscience and the air of
national opinion before it can be cured.

Having someone prophetic in our lives is never
easy. No matter how positive we may believe the
ultimate consequences will be for us, many of us
still shy away from prophetic messages. We
would readily agree with Henry Thoreau: "If
you see someone coming to do you a good
deed, run for your life!" Nonetheless, if we seek
comfort in lieu of the truth we also may bypass
opportunities of real value, of authentic life. In
seeking to avoid pain, we may choose merely to
exist, and eventually we will die without having
ever really lived. As Allen Boesak of South Africa
says: 'We will go before God to be judged, and
God will ask us: 'Where are your wounds?' And
we will say, `We have no wounds.' And God will
ask, 'Was nothing worth fighting for?'"

Maybe we would feel justified in responding to
Boesak: "Oh, I don't have to worry about that
challenge. Look at all my wounds!" But I think
many of our so-called wounds result from a lack
of faith and trust in the Lord. We desire to fill
our arms with our "own-fashioned" crosses

rather than leave them open for the crosses God might wish us to bear.

Seen in this light then, the crosses we bear much of the time are the direct result of our being primarily concerned with something or someone other than God. Even though we believe a lot of the pain we experience is due to our involvement in life and the direct result of reaching out to others (which is sometimes true), it is actually more often than not the product of our putting faith in someone or something less than God. In such instances our worries, insecurities, and preoccupations are due to a lack of faith and a desire to hold on to, or have returned to us, a particular status quo.

For example, we may believe we can only feel secure and happy if our adolescent son behaves as we want, if our elderly parent stays healthy forever, if our friend appreciates us more, if our church follows our ideas now, if . . . . Instead, while such occurrences might be helpful from our point of view, in the spirit of the words and ministry of Jesus true peace will not be produced by getting what we want in every situation. It can only result from placing primary value on what we believe God wants of us (obedience), being in true solidarity with others in life (community), and doing everything in a spirit of love (the greatest law of life).

I think Sheila Cassidy, a physician who was tortured in Chile for treating a revolutionary, points to the heart of the matter when she notes: "If we can come to want only what God wants, then we are in a curious way untouchable; for then loss of property, of good name, or health, or even of life holds no fear, for if that is what God wants, we will be at peace. It is at this point that we become truly free."

Still, what would we do if we really believed this? What if we got up tomorrow morning and could truly forgive others and feel deeply forgiven by God? What if, in the spirit of the early monastic mothers and fathers of the African desert, we were able to begin each day afresh without worry or agenda? What would we do as an encore? If we didn't fill our hearts and heads with worry, the desire to control, or addictions, but simply enjoyed what was before us and found God there, what would we have to complain about most of the time? How would such a life force us to face our limitedness, helplessness, lies, and eventual death? These are the questions prophets help us with.

Prophets point! They point to the fact that it doesn't matter whether pleasure or pain is involved; the only thing that matters is that we seek to be with God in what we do and how we think, feel, and picture ourselves and the world. In other words, we need only to seek and live the truth, because only the truth will set us free.

Prophets challenge us to look at how we are living, to ask ourselves: To what voices am I listening when I form my attitudes and take my actions each day? For instance, I think there is an overwhelming glut of negativity in the media that tells us all is lost. As a result, evil often manifests itself as sensible despair. The evil of omission is not the failure to do impressive things for each other and God. Rather, the evil of omission is not doing the *little* things that we are capable of, the small things God may be calling us to do.

Paradoxically, appreciating the presence of great problems in the world can seem to remove our responsibility to act in good faith rather than serve to call us to a more faithful sense of commitment. We forget that doing what we can is truly a counter-cultural act of faith, especially when surrounded by voices that say: Don't bother; all is lost; no matter what you do, you can't make a difference.

The following story may illustrate this theme more clearly. (As you read it, picture the sparrow as the committed spiritual person and the horseman as the secularist.)

It was a chilly, overcast day when the horseman spied the little sparrow lying on its back in the middle of the road. Reining in his mount, he looked down and inquired of the fragile creature: "Why are you lying upside down like that?"

The sparrow replied: "Oh, early this morning I heard that the sky is going to fall later today."

Upon hearing this, the horseman laughed derisively and said: "And I suppose your spindly legs can hold up the heavens?"

To which the sparrow replied: "One does what one can."

Similarly, Mother Teresa of Calcutta explains that she cannot accept responsibility for the masses. "I look only at the individual. I can only

love one person at a time. Just one, one, one."
And that's the way she began her work in
India—by picking up one dying person.

The question prophets present to us is this: Are
we doing what we can? Their confrontations
with us point out how much more we need to
do, how much more we must act in a loving way
that allows the world to see the face of God in
our actions. They want us to respond to the
challenge Nietzche made to Christians many
years ago. It is unfortunately still a quite valid
challenge today. He said: "I will never believe in
the Christian redeemer until Christians show
me that they themselves have been redeemed."

The Voice of Jesus the Prophet

Reflect on one or both of the following passages in which Jesus speaks prophetically to a friend:

Once while Jesus was standing beside the Lake of Gennesaret, and the crowd was pressing in on him to hear the word of God, he saw two boats there at the shore of the lake; the fishermen had gone out of them and were washing their nets. He got into one of the boats, the one belonging to Simon, and asked him to put out a little way from the shore. Then he sat down and taught the crowds from the boat. When he had finished speaking, he said to Simon, "Put out into the deep water and let down your nets for a catch." Simon answered, "Master, we have worked all night long but have caught nothing. Yet if you say so, I will let down the nets." When they had done this, they caught so many fish that their nets were beginning to break. So they signaled their partners in the other boat to come and help them. And they came and filled both boats, so that they began to sink. But when Simon Peter saw it, he fell down at Jesus' knees, saying, "Go away from me, Lord, for I am a sinful man!" For he and all who were with him were amazed at the catch of fish that they had taken; and so also were James and John, sons of Zebedee, who were partners with Simon. Then Jesus said to Simon, "Do not be afraid; from now on you will be catching people" (Lk 5:1-10).

Jesus' initial encounter with Peter was more than a meeting between a wonderworker and an amazed onlooker. In Jesus, Peter discovered someone who caused him to look into himself and see clearly for the first time. Peter's response was twofold: to admit who he was, and then to embark on a new path to discover who he could become.

- ◆ As you encounter Jesus the prophet in this passage, what do you discover about yourself?

- ◆ What invitation to grow do you hear Jesus the prophet offering you?

A Samaritan woman came to draw water, and Jesus said to her, "Give me a drink." (His disciples had gone to the city to buy food.)

The Samaritan woman said to him, "How is it that you, a Jew, ask a drink of me, a woman of Samaria? (Jews do not share things in common with Samaritans.)

Jesus answered her, "If you knew the gift of God, and who it is that is saying to you, 'Give me a drink,' you would have asked him, and he would have given you living water."

The woman said to him, "Sir, you have no bucket, and the well is deep. Where do you get that living water? Are you greater than our ancestor Jacob, who gave us the well, and with his sons and his flocks drank from it?"

Jesus said to her, "Everyone who drinks of this water will be thirsty again, but those who drink of the water that I will give them will never be thirsty. The water that I will give will become in them a spring of water gushing up to eternal life."

The woman said to him, "Sir, give me this water, so that I may never be thirsty or have to keep coming here to draw water."

Jesus said to her, "Go, call your husband, and come back."

The woman answered him, "I have no husband."

Jesus said to her, "You are right in saying, 'I have no husband,' for you have five husbands, and the one you have now is not your husband. What you have said is true!"

The woman said to him, "Sir, I see that you are a prophet. . . ."

The Samaritan woman discovered in Jesus not only a person who could see through her facade but someone who recognized her true need, her thirst for living water. In response she opened herself to Jesus, saying, "Give me this water," and then went off to proclaim him to her neighbors.

◆ As you encounter Jesus the prophet in this passage, what in you is thirsty for the living water he offers?

◆ Where does Jesus the prophet direct you to go to find the living water?

Recognizing the Prophets in Our Lives

◆ Who do you know living an honest, courageous life guided by truth and compassion? How does this person's presence affect you?

◆ Who in your life helps to bring to the surface inner conflicts or hidden tensions? How does he or she do this?

◆ Who helps you distinguish between your "own-fashioned" crosses and those that God might wish you to bear? How does he or she do this?

◆ Who calls you to live each day afresh without worry?

◆ If there is no one in your life who serves as a prophet, what sources—liturgies, books, public figures, and so on—speak to you in a prophetic way?

Being a Prophet and Friend

◆ A prophet is someone who points. What qualities have you been given that allow you to point toward God? How could you, in the context of your friendships, be a more effective pointer toward God?

◆ A prophet is someone who offers us a mirror to see into ourselves. How do you do that for your friends?

◆ Recall a time when you tried to be a prophet for a friend. What was the response?

◆ When you speak as a prophet to a friend, do your words direct the other to his or her real need, or do they reflect your own desires and needs in the relationship?

◆ What are your feelings about being a prophet? How comfortable is the prophetic voice for you? What are the relationships in which God calls you to be a prophet?

Journal Exercises

◆ Remember a time when a friend served as a prophet for you. In your friend's voice, write the words he or she spoke to you. Then write your immediate reaction at the time. What are your feelings now about the conversation?

◆ Write a dialogue between God and you about your being a prophet.

FOUR

The Cheerleader

Comfort, O comfort my people,
says your God.

◆ Isaiah 40:1

A friend is the hope of the heart.

◆ Ralph Waldo
Emerson

We all need cheerleaders. Ironically, this may be one of the most controversial suggestions I could make with respect to friendship. It is easy to accept the fact that we need people to be prophetic in our lives. We can all recognize how easy it is to lose our way in our desire to control our own destinies or to be secure. We all share a tendency to deny our death and insulate ourselves from God's call to act justly, to love tenderly, and to walk humbly (Mi 6:8). But to say that we need cheerleaders is quite a different matter!

I recently attended a college basketball game and was struck by three things about the cheerleaders. The first thing is that cheerleaders always smile. This occurred to me midway through the second half when the home team was down by about forty points. When they finished their cheer, every one of them had an ear-to-ear grin. It was as if they were saying, "Just wait till after this time-out. We'll score fifty points in a row and win!" Friends who take

the voice of cheerleaders are like that. They
smile no matter what is going wrong. They have
absolutely no doubt about us, even when we
think the situation is hopeless.

Another thing I have noticed about the cheerleaders is that they do tricks. They do somersaults
and backflips, make human pyramids, and perform marvelous balancing acts. Cheerleader
friends are like that. They are willing to stand on
their heads if necessary to get us to pay attention
to what they're saying. They are persistent and
dedicated to making us see ourselves through
their eyes.

When cheerleaders come out on the floor they
often get the crowd to repeat what they're saying. "Gimme a W . . . Gimme an I . . . Gimme
a N . . . !" they shout. Sometimes friends resort
to the same strategy: "You know you're a good
person, don't you? You know how dedicated
you are, don't you?" Like the crowd at a game,
we respond to each question as instructed. And
it really makes a difference.

Some might say that to encourage this type of
friend is to run the risk of narcissism and denial.
However, to balance the prophetic voices and to
let us see the reflection of the loving face of God

more readily in the world, we also need unabashed, enthusiastic, unconditional acceptance by certain people in our lives. Prophecy can and should instill appropriate guilt to break through the crusts of our denial. But guilt cannot sustain us for long. While guilt will push us to do good things because they are right, love encourages us to do the right thing because it is natural.

When we are in pain, the first person to turn to is not the prophet. During difficult times we need loving support so we don't lose perspective. At the end of a discouraging, hurtful day, supportive friends can hold us in their hearts and help us remember we are loved and lovable.

In *Seeking Perspective* I tease people:

> [We all] need the kind of individuals who in response to our complaints about others, give us so much support that we almost feel guilty. And when we express some annoyance at a person or persons, they say something to the effect: You are totally right and they are totally wrong. As a matter of fact, I am getting on my knees this very moment to pray for their early happy death!

Behind such teasing banter there are serious points that deserve emphasis: We can't go it alone. We need a balance of support. We need encouragement and acceptance as much as we need the criticism and feedback that are difficult to hear. Burnout is just around the corner if we don't have people who see our gifts clearly and are always ready to encourage us. We need these cheerleaders to be there for us when we are involved with people who make unrealistic demands on us and when our own crazy expectations for ourselves threaten to pull us down.

I do recognize that to have the cheerleader without the prophet may lead us to project the blame for everything on others; we may become too self-righteous to recognize and admit our own mistakes. This would be a very dangerous situation. Yet, to have our lives filled with prophecy without the presence of God's mercy and love as it is reflected in friends who get joy out of seeing the footprints of God in our personality, is to set the stage for skepticism, sarcasm, defeatism, and despair. Such attitudes cannot help but lead us away from religious and social involvement, because we become so spiritually and emotionally tired that there seems to be no energy left to continue.

Another problem with which the supportive people in our community of friends help us to deal is the emotional drain that results from the angry, hypersensitive, passive-aggressive, and overall needy behavior of some people whom we serve, with whom we work, or who are supposed to be supporting us. Today, so many people, having come from dysfunctional families, are burdened with problems. Having to absorb continually the negativity or demanding behavior of others can slowly and almost indiscernibly sap our energy. It can lead to disastrous results if left unchecked.

A number of years ago a large search was undertaken for a chancellor for a major university system. After a long and arduous process, a man was chosen and took the position, only to resign after less than a year in office. When asked about this, he said that it wasn't anything major that was overwhelming. It was the "gnats" that got to him. The constant bickering, complaints, obstructions, minor hostilities, hypersensitivity, and other such stresses sapped his energy and made him feel overwhelmed, under-appreciated, and drained of creativity.

I didn't fully understand his situation until it happened to me a number of years ago. I was scheduled to go to Canada to lead a series of workshops for a group of teachers who were undergoing a great deal of stress. Just before leaving, I made a mistake in how I handled something at work. In response to this, a co-worker unleashed various levels of anger—open sarcasm, negative comments to others, and a disrespectful personal memo.

This episode bothered me even though I tried to handle it with calm and poise. I finally realized its full impact on the morning of the first workshop I was to lead. Upon waking, I rose, sat on the edge of my bed, and realized I felt beaten and upset. I thought to myself: My heart is so tired; how will I ever be able to reach out to those counting on me today?

I could see that I set up my very active schedule with the unrealistic expectation that I would never run into problems with the people who were hired to support my efforts. I also had conveniently forgotten the difficulty I normally have in dealing with people's anger and the undue concern I still have about my image. (These things always serve to remind me of my continued need for God's grace and greater humility.)

Later that morning, I was thankful that when I saw the faces of the teachers with whom I was to work, I did become energized by their deep sense of commitment. I was then able to respond competently and from the heart with a sense of honesty.

Nonetheless, I knew the issue was not resolved, and when I got home I shared the episode with my wife. I explained why I felt the person who was so angry with me touched a sensitive chord. I mentioned that if I had another job opportunity, I might be tempted to commit the sin of taking it even though I still felt called to be in my current position. I felt like running away from a situation where, instead of support, I was feeling the pain of "little knives in my back." I was also feeling sorry for myself. I kept thinking, "Where does this person get the time and energy to be such a pain?"

My wife's response was: "You know you are a good person, and yet you are giving away too much power to those who are angry with you. It's not fair to you or to those who count on you. You may have made a mistake in judgment, but you didn't deserve the amount of anger and certainly not the disrespect you received as a result. A responsible adult should have given you the benefit of the doubt or at the very least come to speak with you instead of behaving like an angry two-year-old. Try to recognize, though, that he may not even realize how he is acting. You may have to confront him on his lack of respect if he acts like this in the future. But you know he may not understand. After all, aren't you always advising people to have low expectations and high hopes when dealing with others?"

Her comments were just what I needed to hear to help me regain necessary perspective and feel appropriate self-love. She helped me to encounter the love of God during a very difficult time. With her support I could once again agree with W. S. Gilbert's comment: "You have no idea what a poor opinion I have of myself, and how little I deserve it!"

So, while having buoyantly supportive friends may seem like a luxury, make no mistake about it, it is a necessity that is not to be taken lightly. The interpersonal roads of time are strewn with well-meaning people who tried to survive without such support. Encouragement is a gift that should be treasured in today's stressful, anxious, complex world, because the seeds of involvement and the seeds of burnout are the same. To be involved is to risk. To risk without the presence of solidly supportive friends is foolhardy and dangerous. Warm friends represent the incarnational love of God in our lives and remind us, in the words of Paul Tillich, that faith is best defined as the courage to accept acceptance.

The Voice of Jesus the Cheerleader

Reflect on one or both of these passages in which Jesus offers encouragement and affirmation to a friend:

Now when Jesus came into the district of Caesarea Philippi, he asked his disciples, "Who do people say that the Son of Man is?" And they said, "Some say John the Baptist, but others Elijah, and still others Jeremiah or one of the prophets." He said to them, "But who do you say that I am?" Simon Peter answered, "You are the Messiah, the Son of the living God." And Jesus answered him, "Blessed are you, Simon son of Jonah! For flesh and blood has not revealed this to you, but my Father in heaven. And I tell you, you are Peter, and on this rock I will build my church, and the gates of Hades will not prevail against it" (Mt 16: 13-18).

Jesus' question is picked up by Peter, who always seems willing to go out on a limb. In response to the risk Peter takes Jesus says, "Blessed are you, Simon!" In reflecting on this passage we usually focus on Peter's act of faith.

But Jesus' words should not be overlooked. He offers Peter the encouragement and praise he needs to accept his mission.

◆ Focus on a situation in which you have been discouraged. Allow Jesus to speak to you and say, "Blessed are you!" Hear him speak your name. Allow him to offer you the encouragement you need.

While he was at Bethany in the house of Simon the leper, as he sat at the table, a woman came with an alabaster jar of very costly ointment of nard, and she broke open the jar and poured the ointment on his head. But some were there who said to one another in anger, "Why was the ointment wasted in this way? For this ointment could have been sold for more than three hundred denarii and the money given to the poor." And they scolded her. But Jesus said, "Let her alone; why do you trouble her? She has performed a good service for me. For you always have the poor with you, and you can show kindness to them whenever you wish; but you will not always have me. She has done what she could; she has anointed my body beforehand for its burial. Truly I tell you, wherever the good news is proclaimed in the whole world, what she

has done will be told in remembrance of her"
(Mk 14: 3-9).

What the woman in this passage did was certainly risky. She burst into the house of a
powerful religious leader and interrupted his
dinner with Jesus. Then she took an expensive
jar of oil and poured it upon Jesus without
regard for the cost. All for no apparent reason.

Simon the Pharisee rebuked her. But Jesus saw
beyond the conventions of society—even
beyond the beautiful gesture—into her heart.
When she was most vulnerable, under criticism,
perhaps even doubting herself, Jesus praised her
for her actions, affirming their worth.

◆ Jesus says of this woman, "She has done what
  she could." Reflect on a time you were criti-
  cized by others or by yourself and allow Jesus
  to say to you, "You have done what you
  could."

Recognizing the Cheerleaders in Our Lives

◆ Who offers you unabashed, enthusiastic,
  unconditional acceptance when you need it?

What effect does this person have on you?

◆ Who knows your gifts and helps you remember them when you're headed for burnout? How does he or she do this?

◆ What happens to you when you are plagued by other people's anger, hypersensitivity, or passive-aggressive behavior? Can you recognize these signs, or do you need someone else to point them out to you? How can you show your openness to someone who does this for you?

◆ How does it take courage for you to accept the acceptance of others?

◆ When there is no one available to be a cheerleader, what do you do? Are there any other ways to find the support you need?

Being a Cheerleader and Friend

◆ A cheerleader is someone who encourages. What qualities have you been given that help you to encourage others? How could you, in the context of your friendships, be a more effective voice of encouragement?

◆ How do you feel about offering compliments
   to others? What do you think the difference
   is between an authentic and a phony compliment? How do you feel when someone offers
   you a compliment?

◆ Can you recall a time when you tried to be a
   cheerleader for a friend? What was the response?

◆ Are there any obstacles or hesitancies that
   keep you from offering the encouragement
   that your friends need, for example, preoccu-
   pation with self, fear of sounding foolish, not
   knowing if the time is right? How can you
   better deal with these?

◆ What are your feelings, both positive and
   negative, about being a cheerleader? Is it a
   comfortable role for you? Are there any relationships in which God calls you to be a
   cheerleader?

Journal Exercises

◆ Recall something encouraging that has been
   said to you recently. Try to write it in the
   words of the person who spoke to you. Then
   write what your immediate reaction was.
   What are your feelings now as you remember
   the conversation?

◆ Make a list of the most encouraging people you know. Place a quality next to each name that expresses what makes them good at this. Then make a list of people who need your encouragement and write next to each name what you would like to say to each one.

FIVE

The Harasser

The angel of the Lord came a second time, touched Elijah and said, "Get up and eat, otherwise the journey will be too much for you."

◆ 1 Kings 19: 7

The best mirror is an old friend.

◆ George Herbert

*T*he first book of Kings tells the story of the prophet Elijah fleeing from Queen Jezebel. She has vowed to kill him to avenge the deaths of the priests of Baal in Elijah's famous showdown with them (1 Kgs 18:20-19:10). Elijah flees into the desert, but after a day's journey he is exhausted and in despair. He lies down under the broom tree and prays that God will take his life. God sends an angel to provide food and drink. After eating, Elijah lies down again. The angel comes again, telling him, "Get up and eat, otherwise the journey will be too much for you."

While in the first instance we might see the angel as an angel of mercy, on the second visit the angel becomes a figure of the next type of friend we will consider—the harasser. Along with the prophet and cheerleader, we all need, from time to time, the harasser. This type of friend can help us to face the same danger that Elijah was about to give in to: on the way to taking God seriously, we may instead end up taking ourselves too seriously.

Being a harasser may not sound too appealing. The word harassment has strong negative connotations, and justifiably so. Perhaps it brings to mind sexual harassment or the verbal abuse children inflict on one another in the schoolyard. I obviously don't mean it in those ways. But if we look at the negative meaning of the term, we can get at the positive meaning it can have, through the back door, if you will.

Harassment is degrading, demeaning, and humiliating. It takes an attribute of a person, often something to do with his or her physical appearance or a personality characteristic, and treats this part of the person as if it were the whole. A person is then identified with this part of the body or this characteristic. "Four-eyes" or "Nitwit" are some of the less degrading but still hurtful examples that come to mind.

How can we possibly harass people in a positive way? Positive harassment is a kind of "harassing back." We need it when we have been harassing ourselves, putting ourselves down or blowing a negative experience out of proportion. Positive harassment is not degrading but upgrading; rather than demeaning it helps us find meaning; instead of humiliating us, it points us toward true humility.

When we are taking ourselves too seriously, the harasser helps us to adjust our perspective. When we are looking at just one aspect of our life or our experience, the harasser helps us to see the whole. The most effective tool the harasser has is humor. Not sarcastic or cutting humor, but gentle humor. When we are getting too caught up in ourselves, the harasser will follow our lead and exaggerate the situation even more, sometimes taking it to the point of absurdity.

A number of years ago I gave a lecture to a particular group of undergraduates and it instantly went awry. To make matters worse, I become anxious in such situations and tend to speed up. So, even though I just started teaching the course, by the end of the class period I felt I had already presented the main points of my entire semester's notes! After the class was over, I stepped out into the hall feeling awful. One of my colleagues, who is also a psychologist and happened to be standing at the end of the hallway, saw my face and was at my side in an instant. (You know how they love to treat their own!)

He said: "You look depressed. Why is that?"

"I just gave a presentation and it went terribly from the beginning; it sank like a rock in water."

"But why are you depressed?" he repeated.

"They were so bored that they continually checked their watches to see if their batteries were run down!"

Again he asked: "But why are you depressed?"

"I couldn't believe how disinterested they were. They did something that I didn't think was statistically possible—they actually yawned in unison!"

He steadfastly asked again, "But why are you depressed?"

By then I was not only depressed but also furious at him. I growled, "After all I have told you, why shouldn't I be depressed?"

"Because five seconds after you left the room, they probably forgot what your name was."

To this I laughingly exclaimed, "My goodness! Isn't there any easier way we could put this in perspective?"

This story points out how I was guilty of the sin of negative grandiosity. I was taking myself so seriously that I was pulling myself down.

When singer-activist Joan Baez was asked her opinion about Thomas Merton, one of the things she said was that he was different from many of the gurus she had encountered in her travels. She said that although Merton took important things seriously in his life, he didn't take himself too seriously. She indicated that he knew how to laugh at situations and particularly at himself. In many instances we fail to be like Merton, and we lose perspective because of it.

One of the best biblical examples of harassment is the story of the Canaanite woman told in Matthew 15:21-28. She was a pagan woman who approached Jesus seeking a cure for her daughter. Jesus put her off saying that he had come for the children of Israel. When she persisted, Jesus said, "It is not fair to take the children's food and throw it to dogs." But she responded, "Even the dogs eat the crumbs that fall from their master's table!" Jesus was won over and praised her faith. He also healed her daughter.

This story has been the subject of great debate in Christian history. Some say that Jesus knew all along what he was going to do and was just testing the woman. Others think that she persuaded him, that she made him change his mind. Both opinions can be mined for rich insights. But let's take the second one for now.

From this perspective we could say that Jesus was taking his mission to the Israelites very seriously. From her point of view, he was too serious about it. So she takes his very serious statement about not throwing the children's food to the dogs and exaggerates it. In doing so, she changes his perspective. She gets to him to look beyond the mission to the person of her little girl. She harasses him into curing her daughter! We can almost see the smile on Jesus' face as he gives in.

Harassers can win us over with their gentle humor. They help us to laugh at ourselves. In so doing they help us avoid the emotional burnout that comes from placing unrealistic expectations on ourselves; we don't have to perform perfectly all the time. Harassers change our viewpoint in those times when people don't follow our guidance or appreciate what we do for them. This type of friend helps us regain and maintain perspective, so we don't unnecessarily waste valuable energy. This kind of friend is a gift for which we can be thankful.

The Voice of Jesus the Harasser

Reflect on one or both of these passages in which Jesus challenges a friend to see things differently:

And early in the morning he came walking toward them on the sea. But when the disciples saw him walking on the sea, they were terrified, saying, "It is a ghost!" And they cried out in fear. But immediately Jesus spoke to them and said, "Take heart, it is I; do not be afraid."

Peter answered him, "Lord, if it is you, command me to come to you on the water." He said, "Come." So Peter got out of the boat, started walking on the water, and came toward Jesus. But when he noticed the strong wind, he became frightened, and beginning to sink, he cried out, "Lord, save me!" Jesus immediately reached out his hand and caught him, saying to him, "You of little faith, why did you doubt?" (Mt 14: 25-31).

While this passage may not perfectly fit the type of friendship I have called "the harasser," it does help us to see how Jesus can help us change our perspective when we take ourselves too seriously.

◆ Peter forgets that his ability to walk on the water does not depend upon himself but upon Jesus. What situations in your life are like this? Place yourself on the water with Peter. As you begin to sink, allow Jesus to reach out and grasp your hand. What does he say to you?

Now as they went on their way, he entered a certain village, where a woman named Martha welcomed him into her home. She had a sister named Mary, who sat at the Lord's feet and listened to what he was saying. But Martha was distracted by her many tasks; so she came to him and asked, "Lord, do you not care that my sister has left me to do all the work by myself? Tell her then to help me." But the Lord answered her, "Martha, Martha, you are worried and distracted by many things; there is need of only one thing. Mary has chosen the better part, which will not be taken away from her" (Lk 10: 38-42).

Martha took herself very seriously. Perhaps she learned as a child from her mother what a good hostess was supposed to do, and she was determined to do it. Mary would have learned the same thing, but she wasn't following the rules. So Martha turns to Jesus, expecting that he will

take her side and send Mary to the kitchen to
help her. But Jesus won't be bound by social
conventions either. He gently reminds Martha
that she has lost her perspective and gotten her
priorities mixed up. Interestingly, Luke doesn't
tell us what Martha did next. Did she walk off
in a huff, or did she find a new sense of freedom
and sit down with Mary to listen to Jesus?

◆ Just as Martha was feeling the burden of hos-
pitality, our life and work can sometimes feel
burdensome. This is often when we lose perspective. Unburden yourself to Jesus. Feel free
to tell him what's weighing you down. Then
be still and listen to what he says.

Recognizing the Harassers in Our Lives

◆ Who knows you well enough to recognize
when you are taking yourself too seriously?
What does he or she do about it? What effect
does this have on you?

◆ How do you respond to the harasser's gentle
humor? When is this style of friendship helpful to you? When is it unhelpful?

◆ Who helps you to laugh at yourself? What tech-
niques does he or she use to help you do this?

◆ What do you appreciate about the harassers in your life? How do you express your gratitude to them?

Being a Harasser and Friend

◆ How does this style of friendship fit with your personality?

◆ How do you respond when you observe a friend losing perspective or taking himself or herself too seriously?

◆ How do you use humor in your relationships? What do you do if your attempts at gentle humor come across as sarcasm?

Journal Exercises

◆ Recall a time when someone used humor to help you avoid to taking yourself too seriously. What was your immediate reaction? What are your feelings now as you remember the conversation?

◆ Make a list of the people you know with the best sense of humor. Describe how each one's humor affects you and why.

SIX

The Spiritual Guide

Where two or three are gathered in my name, I am there among them.

◆ *Matthew 18: 20*

Whoever travels without a guide needs two hundred years for two days' journey.

◆ *Jalaluddin Rumi,*
Sufi sage

*T*he three types of friends we've looked at so far are each part of a necessary community. The prophet enhances our sense of single-heartedness. The cheerleader generously showers us with the support we need. The harasser encourages us to maintain a sense of proper perspective. These three, all in their own ways, are spiritual companions.

Spiritual companions are those who, amid the complexity, stress, and even boredom of modern existence, can foster an increase in the development of meaning in our lives. These are the people who call us to be all that we can be without embarrassing us because we presently are where we are. Even if we only see these persons once in a while or speak only rarely of specifically religious matters with them, we gain

a sense of feeling nourished, awake, and recon-
nected to life from them.

While the prophet, the cheerleader, and the
harasser can be spiritual companions, what we'll
be focusing on in this chapter and the next is the
role of that friend who serves *explicitly* as a spiritual guide. In this chapter we'll look at how
spiritual guides help us uncover and deal with
our fears, appreciate what we need to be
detached from, and instill in us a sense of
renewed perspective and enthusiasm. In the
next chapter we'll look at three types of guides.

Recently when I was in Denver to help celebrate the inauguration of a new program in
pastoral counseling, I overheard a member of a
Catholic religious community telling about one
of their sisters who had come to the region
many, many years ago to ask for material support for the community. Her story went like
this:

> The woman religious was dressed in the
> full religious habit of the day and appeared
> at the fence of a farm outside the city lim-
> its of Denver. After she had been standing
> there for a period of time, the man who
> owned the farm spotted her. He walked

down to meet her and asked if he could be of help. She blurted out, "I wonder if you could donate a cow to my community?"

Not being Catholic, he didn't know what to make of the request. But after pausing to scratch his head and reflect for a moment, he smiled, shrugged, and said, "Why not?"

After hearing this reply, and realizing that she hadn't even told the generous farmer anything about her congregation's work before asking for his help, she quickly added, "You know, we have been begging for help for over one hundred years." He retorted with a laugh, "Gee, you'd think by now that you'd have all you need."

When I recall this enjoyable story, I feel a similar sentiment about myself and my own journey in life. My thought is: You would think by now I would have enough of the information and experience I need in order to live a good and vital spiritual life. However, as we all realize, it is not as easy as that.

Life is always changing, and we cannot "go it alone." We need companions on our journey, friends who can serve as spiritual guides. There are three areas of our lives where the presence of a spiritual guide is especially helpful: dealing with our unrecognized and unnecessary fears, appreciating the need for proper detachment, and maintaining a sense of enthusiasm and perspective in a world strained by anxiety and confusion.

Dealing with Our Fears

Fear can be very dangerous. Not only can it lead to an unhealthy desire for withdrawal, but the very fear of fear can lead some people to give up acre after acre of their life. Some find the snapping of twigs so uncomfortable that they abandon the territory of life entirely. At the extreme, as Bertrand Russell aptly points out, fear can lead to aggression; fear is the main source of superstition, and one of the main sources of cruelty. To conquer fear is the beginning of wisdom.

A major role of spiritual guides is to help us discover our fears. They help us ask ourselves: What is the worst thing that can happen if I face my fears?

One of the greatest hidden fears is the anxiety that results when we fail to realize God's unconditional love. We then tend to inflate our self-image in order to counter-balance the lack of self-worth that results from failing to realize God's love for us. We become preoccupied with the image we wish to project to the world. We may invest an inordinate amount of energy trying to be seen as someone who is hardworking, helpful, successful, unique, knowing, loyal, nice, powerful, or acceptable. In such instances, we hold to the erroneous belief that we must hide, at all cost, our anger, pride, deceit, envy, stinginess, fear, self-indulgence, arrogance, or laziness. We hide behind a screen of efforts that prove (to ourselves, others, and God) that we are perfect.

In such cases our fears are not real. They come from failing to believe that our ordinariness is all that matters in the eyes of God. We attempt to fabricate an image in our own and others' eyes because we lack the trust to believe that in God's eyes being simply ourselves (ordinary) is enough. To make matters worse, our response to this lack of faith is often manifested in actions that demonstrate a willful desire to be independent of the Creator or to deny the need for grace. Rabbi Abraham Heschel describes this process poetically:

> After having eaten the forbidden fruit, the Lord sent forth man from paradise, to till the ground from which he was taken. But man, who is more subtle than any other creature that God has made, what did he do? He undertook to build a paradise by his own might, and he is driving God from his paradise.

And so, our guides listen to us carefully and don't accept the manifest content (what we say and do) as being equal to the total content (our actual intentions *plus* our statements and actions). Instead, they search for nuances in what we share with them to help us to uncover some of the voices that are unconsciously guiding our lives, especially the ones that undermine our trust in God and make us hesitant, anxious, fearful, and willful.

Appreciating Detachment

Simone Weil once said that attachment is the great fabricator of illusions; reality can be attained only by someone who is detached. But the subject of detachment is not an easy one to appreciate. Possibly the best way of illustrating the principle is to look at the problem of inordinate attachment reflected in the following story about the proper way to catch monkeys:

Since monkeys are very bright and frenetic, they are difficult to catch without causing them harm. So some people have devised a simple technique to capture them. They empty out gourds, fill them with peanuts, and then patch up the gourds so only a small opening remains in each one. They then attach the gourds to trees and leave the area.

After a while, when they feel safe and all is quiet, the monkeys come down from the trees, stick their hands in the gourds and grab a handful of peanuts. To pull their hands back out and escape, all they need do is let go of the peanuts. But they hold on, screaming with fear and frustration, until the trappers come back and catch them.

The question spiritual guides present us with is: What "peanuts" are we holding on to that are preventing us from experiencing God's peace? As Jesus noted, "Wherever your treasure is, there will your heart be too" (Mt 6:21). What preoccupies and troubles us most of the time? What do we think about the first thing in the morning, as we drive or walk around during the day, and shortly before going to bed? Most often, these are our peanuts, our gods. Spiritual guides teach us proper discernment with respect to our concerns.

In keeping with the following excerpt from Jewish spiritual wisdom, spiritual guides first encourage us to enjoy fully our family, friends, success, food, money, health—all the gifts of God.

The Jerusalem Talmud states that when, after life, we confront ultimate judgment, one of the issues on the table will be whether we denied ourselves the experience of those enjoyments that God made available, and if so, why? God does not play games, making enjoyable pleasures available but then saying we cannot touch them, cannot enjoy them. On the contrary, by denying them, we miss the experience of God's majesty.

However, spiritual guides also point out that if we become so attached to these gifts that we are no longer disciplined in their use and feel we cannot be happy without them, then something is wrong. We are not free anymore.

The apostles who experienced the transfiguration were obviously not expected to close their eyes to the beauty of the experience. (To do so would be to turn their backs on a wonderful gift of God; more than that, it would be an act of ingratitude.) But, on the other hand, neither were they called to set up tents there. Instead, they were expected through this experience of God to be free to carry the experience within them and go out into the unknown future, even to Jerusalem. So, other questions we are asked to grapple with by our spiritual guides are: Are we truly grateful for the people and things God has given us to enjoy in our lives? Are we also willing to let go of them rather than to try to possess, control, or idolize them?

As members of an efficient, frequently insecure, contemporary society, it is often difficult for us to accept the wisdom of the desert. Nonetheless, the following story recounted by Yoshi Nomura aptly summarizes this theme:

> Abba Doulas, the disciple of Abba Bessarion, said, "When we were walking along the sea one day, I was thirsty, so I

said to Abba Bessarion, 'Abba, I am very thirsty.' Then the old man prayed, and said to me, 'Drink from the sea.' The water was sweet when I drank it. And I poured it into a flask, so that I would not be thirsty later. Seeing this, the old man asked me, 'Why are you doing that?' I answered, 'Excuse me, but it's so that I won't be thirsty later on.' Then the old man said, 'God is here, and God is everywhere.'"

Maintaining a Sense of Enthusiasm and Perspective

Spiritual guides also seek out our true inner charism (cf. 1 Cor 12). Our gifts are like sparks that need to be fanned into a flame, not put under a bushel basket. They have been given to us by God to share with others in a spirit of enthusiasm and perspective. To accomplish this, spiritual guides must continually help people discern the distinction between genuine enthusiasm and other emotions that merely mimic it.

For instance, enthusiasm and exhilaration are not the same thing. Exhilaration may be present when we are enthusiastic, but many times it is not. To always expect exhilaration is to make ourselves pleasure-addicts. This in itself will block the development of a deeply enthusiastic attitude. Real enthusiasm can only develop and grow to maturity in a personality that seeks to be free of compulsive behavior, irrational thinking, incorrect imagery, unnecessary negative emotion, and the need for immediate gratification.

A number of years ago I was having lunch with an editor. He told me he could tell the difference between someone who had successfully endured a lot of difficulties in life and someone who had not. When I asked how, he said that someone who had suffered was deeper in his or her emotions; their experience of joy and sadness was not superficial.

Spiritual guides help us avoid a surface exhilaration or a pseudo-positive thinking mode. They remind us that a grateful, open, assertive, and free approach to a world opens up opportunities for the deep personal joy and peace that is even possible amid the reality of suffering.

Author John Gardner aptly pointed out a number of years ago that we are all continually faced with great opportunities, brilliantly disguised as insoluble problems. The point he is making is that when our eyes are opened and the "Aha!" experience dawns, we are able to put things in perspective and embrace enthusiasm. Thus, annoyances remain annoyances and don't move into the realm of preoccupations that pull us down; we are able to appreciate the gift of perspective in our lives.

Perspective and enthusiasm go hand-in-hand. You can't have one without the other. Perspective loosens up our perceptions so as to allow the important issues to take precedence in a world frequently caught up in false agenda. These false agenda blur the line between what is essential (relationships, peace, love) and what isn't (inordinate power, concern with image, competition, accomplishments).

The following letter, written by a first-year college student to her father during the middle of her second semester, delightfully points this out. Prior to receiving this note, her father was totally preoccupied with her success in college. He was worried because she didn't do well in her first semester and was concerned she would flunk out during the second semester and the money he had invested in her education would be wasted. He had forgotten that performance in courses is only a partial measure of learning;

moreover, there is much more to the total college experience than just grades.

Despite her youth, this young woman knew this better than he, and so was able to teach him an important lesson on perspective:

> Dear Dad,
>
> Everything is going well here at college this semester, so you can stop worrying. I am very, very happy now, and you would love Ichabod. He is a wonderful, wonderful man and our first three months of marriage have been blissful.
>
> And more good news, Dad. The drug rehab program we are both in just told us that the twins who are due soon will not be addicted at birth.

Having read this, her father then turned the page with trepidation.

On the other side of the note it said:

```
Now, Dad, there actually is
no Ichabod. I'm not married
or pregnant. And I have
never abused drugs. But I
did get a D in chemistry,
so keep things in perspec-
tive!
```

Spiritual guides help us open up to life so we can more clearly reflect on the perils to, and the seeds of, perspective and enthusiasm. Spiritual guides thus enable us to recapture the simplicity that is born of seeing life not merely as something to succeed at but as something to experience fully and freely, as God wishes. This undertaking must be a daily prayerful effort and supported by others who are graced and gifted, if we are not to lose our way, a real possibility given the demands and unhealthy lures of modern life.

The Voice of Jesus, the Spiritual Guide

Reflect on one or both of these passages in which Jesus challenges a friend to see things differently:

Jesus took with him Peter and John and James, and went up on the mountain to pray. And while he was praying, the appearance of his face changed, and his clothes became dazzling white. Suddenly they saw two men, Moses and Elijah, talking to him. They appeared in glory and were speaking of his departure, which he was about to accomplish at Jerusalem. Now Peter and his companions were weighed down with sleep; but since they had stayed awake, they saw his glory and the two men who stood with him. Just as they were leaving him, Peter said to Jesus, "Master, it is good for us to be here; let us make three dwellings, one for you, one for Moses, and one for Elijah"—not knowing what he said. While he was saying this, a cloud came and overshadowed them; and they were terrified as they entered the cloud. Then from the cloud came a voice that said, "This is

my Son, my Chosen; listen to him!" When the
voice had spoken, Jesus was found alone. And
they kept silent and in those days told no one
any of the things they had seen (Lk 9: 28-36).

One characteristic of a spiritual guide is the
openness to share his or her own relationship
with God with friends. Jesus brings Peter,
James, and John with him to the mountaintop
to do just that. His presence helps them over-
come their fears at this wondrous event.

Caught up in the experience, Peter wishes to
build three tents there. He doesn't want the
moment to end; he wants to stay on top of the
mountain. But, having prepared them for what
lies ahead, Jesus leads them back down the mountain to the ordinary level of human experience.

◆ Reflect on a mountaintop experience of your
   own. Give thanks for this experience and pray
   for the ability to recognize God in the ordinary as well as the extraordinary.

But Mary stood weeping outside the tomb. As
she wept, she bent over to look into the tomb;
and she saw two angels in white, sitting where
the body of Jesus had been lying, one at the head
and the other at the feet. They said to her,

"Woman, why are you weeping?" She said to
them, "They have taken away my Lord, and I do
not know where they have laid him." When she
had said this, she turned around and saw Jesus
standing there, but she did not know that it was
Jesus. Jesus said to her, "Woman, why are you
weeping? Whom are you looking for?"
Supposing him to be the gardener, she said to
him, "Sir, if you have carried him away, tell me
where you have laid him, and I will take him
away." Jesus said to her, "Mary!" She turned and
said to him in Hebrew, "Rabbouni!" (which
means Teacher). Jesus said to her, "Do not hold
on to me, because I have not yet ascended to the
Father. But go to my brothers and say to them,
'I am ascending to my Father and your Father,
to my God and your God.'" Mary Magdalene
went and announced to the disciples, "I have
seen the Lord"; and she told them that he had
said these things to her (Jn 20: 11-18).

◆ Still filled with grief at the loss of Jesus and
   wondering what the disappearance of his
   body could mean, Mary stood weeping in
   the garden. Enter into your own place of
   confusion, of grief, or of loss. Stay in that
   place with her for as long as you wish.

◆ With Mary, notice a man whom you suppose
   to be the gardener. Ask with her, "Sir, if you

have carried him away, tell me where you have
laid him?" Then hear Jesus say your name.
What do you do?

◆ After a time, Jesus says to you, "Do not hold
on to me, but go to my brothers and sisters."
To whom do you go?

◆ Are there things in your life, perhaps good
things, to which you may be overly attached?
Give thanks for these things. Seek an attitude
of gratefulness for them and pray to be able to
let go of your excessive attachment to them.

Recognizing the Spiritual Guides in Our Lives

◆ Who among your friends is able to listen not
only to the "manifest content" (what you say
and do), but also the "total content" (your
intentions as well as what you say and do)?
How is this person a spiritual guide for you?

◆ When you are struggling with fears, who
helps you to name them and reflect on your
particular way of handling them?

◆ Who helps you recognize the things that you
are clinging to that keep you from experiencing God's peace?

◆ Who helps you recognize the unique gifts you possess and your special way of caring, the sources of true enthusiasm?

◆ If no one offers you the type of support described in the above questions, who is someone with whom you would like to develop this kind of relationship?

Being a Spiritual Guide and Friend

◆ How do you try to help friends deal with their fears? What difference do you think you make to them?

◆ Are you more inclined to recommend your own opinion on what your friends should do or to help them sort out the possible options? Which approach do you think is better? Why?

◆ How are you able to help your friends own their particular gifts and reflect on their lives in light of these gifts?

Journal Exercises

◆ If there is someone you consider to be a spiritual guide or companion, reflect on the particular qualities of that person which enable you to share your spiritual life with him or her.

◆ Write the names of one or more of your friends, and then list the special gifts of each person.

◆ The questions below touch on some of the important attributes of a spiritual guide. Keep in mind that you need not possess all of these attributes to be of genuine help to another. Reflect on your gifts in light of these questions.

—How good a listener am I?

—How sensitive am I to the emotional content of what others say to me?

—How well am I able to reflect back to others what I hear them saying?

—Is prayer and reflection on my spirituality a consistent part of my life?

—Am I comfortable about sharing my spiritual life with others?

—Do I try to learn more about spirituality through books, tapes, conversations, classes, and so on?

SEVEN

Types of Guides

If I take the wings of the dawn,
if I settle at the farthest limits of
  the sea,
even there your hand shall
  guide me.

◆ *Psalm 139:10*
   (NAB)

Anyone without a soul friend is
like a body without a head.

◆ *St. Brigit*

*T*here is a story told about the great desert hermit Anthony's observations of another monk named Paphnutius:

*O*ne day Paphnutius was standing on the bank of a river observing a man stuck in the knee-deep mud. As some others came to try and help him out, Paphnutius noticed that the more they tried, the deeper the man sank, until he was up to his neck! While Paphnutius doesn't say what lessons he saw in this little incident, Anthony implies that Paphnutius was pointing out the dangers of a guide who tries to solve another's problems. Anthony is impressed with Paphnutius's powers of observation and says of him, "Here is a real man, who can care for souls and save them!"

Anthony's comment highlights the fact that sometimes a spiritual guide can do more harm than good. That is why we must choose a guide carefully. Speaking about the importance of selecting our guide carefully, St. John of the Cross writes, "A person, desiring to advance in recollection and perfection, [should] take care into whose hands he entrusts himself, for the disciple will become like the master."

This chapter seeks to offer some help in the process of finding a spiritual guide by examining three types of guides that might be available to us and offering suggestions on how to find a spiritual guide. The three types we will discuss are the spiritual director; the spiritual *amma* or *abba;* and books and places.

Spiritual Directors

The focus of the encounter with this type of guide is our relationship with God and all this entails. We meet with our spiritual director on a regular basis and are primarily concerned with strengthening our covenant with God in a way that results in our being more integrated as persons and more open to interacting with and serving others.

Carolyn Gratton describes a spiritual director as a co-listener to the voice of the Spirit, who is already at work guiding each of our lives:

> *H*e or she has the task, within that already intentional relationship, of paying attention to God's presence in the life of this other person, of attempting to make conscious the ongoing dialogue with God that gives meaning to that life. . . . Directors aim at integrating prayer and life, contemplation and action, faith and justice, in their own lives as well as those of their directees.

The director not only listens to us, but also with us. The director becomes a third party in our ongoing dialogue with God. Margaret Guenther describes the task of the director as "holy listening." It is a relationship of presence and attentiveness.

Guenther also compares the role of a director to that of a midwife. Like the midwife, the spiritual director is "present to another in a time of vulnerability, working in areas that are deep and intimate. It is a relationship of trust and mutual respect." Like a midwife, a spiritual director assists in a natural event. Just as birth is not a clinical problem to be solved but a natural and very human reality, so too is spiritual growth.

Both the midwife and the director offer guidance, encouragement, and at times, confrontation. "The midwife invites questions, and then takes time to answer them," Guenther notes. Helping the birth-giver feel comfortable with herself and the process is an essential part of her role. The midwife can offer real encouragement because she is familiar with the process. She sees what the mother cannot. "She knows the transition period—a time of desolation, of seemingly unmanageable pain and nausea—to be a sign of breakthrough and great progress." And the midwife has learned the delicate art of confrontation. "To confront is quite literally to face another; in midwifery, both physical and spiritual, the helper's loving detachment can bring clarity to the situation," Guenther adds.

In many cases those filling the role of spiritual director have received both a call from God and formal preparation through studies in spirituality, forms of prayer, sacred scriptures, theology, and applied psychology. However, this need not always be the case. The charism of being a director is freely given by God to whomever the Creator pleases. As a result, we sometimes see people in this role who have not actually gone through formal or specific education to prepare for the work. Yet they have been given the gift, and the Lord draws to them people who are in search of a more intimate relationship with God.

Conversely, there are some well-qualified directors who clearly do not have the call; their emotional energy is primarily directed at trying to shore up their own psychological defenses and meeting their own needs. Thus little is left to put at the service of those who are seeking their guidance.

The choice of someone to fill the role of spiritual director in our life can sometimes be quite difficult. The first thing we must do is approach the search with faith. Pray for a director and trust that in God's providence we will find one. But then, "having prayed as if everything depends on God," as the saying goes, "we should act as if everything depends on us."

The first and most practical thing we can do is ask for recommendations from people whose judgment we respect in this area—friends knowledgeable about spiritual direction, members of the pastoral team serving the parish, staff in diocesan offices of adult spirituality or family life. In many cases the spiritually mature people in our lives can lead us to someone who can help us develop our prayer life.

Among qualities that we should look for in the director, Thomas Dubay highlights prayerfulness, rootedness in the church, adequate knowledge of spirituality and theology, sound judgment and life experience, some awareness of psychology; the director should be one to whom we can comfortably relate. While it is difficult to find all of these qualities in one person, this list can help us assess the particular strengths and weaknesses of those we may be considering.

The process of selecting a director is difficult and may take several tries. We need to remember to be prayerful, prudent, patient, and persistent.

Spiritual Ammas and Abbas

Spiritual ammas and abbas comprise the next type of guide that we may need at certain times in our lives. The terms *amma* and *abba* mean "mother" and "father." The essential point to remember about this type of spiritual friend is that persons such as these are usually only called upon at certain turning points in our lives. They help us discern a major change in direction, by checking on the way we have understood our calling or reviewing the focus of our life's work.

For instance, when the author Henri Nouwen was teaching at Harvard Divinity School, I went to visit him when I was feeling both a sense of burnout and a call to become more open to God in my life. I asked him how I could better nourish my relationship with God and my role as a pastoral psychologist working primarily with people in ministry. Both my questions and his responses were very important at this point in my life; they were orienting points at an essential developmental stage for me.

The important factors to remember with respect to seeking out a wise and holy person to ask for help at crucial junctures in life are these:

1. We should seek such special assistance only when there is a real need and we have already utilized and found somewhat wanting all the existing supports in our lives, including our own personal resources (problem-solving schemas, reflection, prayer, and so forth).

2. We need to be serious in our request for information and not just inquisitive.

Some people continually ask for a word from spiritual figures without weighing the gravity of their request.

3. We must take special care to select someone who will be of real benefit to us at this point. There is an old Russian proverb: The hammer shatters glass but forges steel. A sage who can be of real help to one person at certain junctures in life may be of no assistance at another point or never be of help at all to other types of individuals who seek assistance. Only Jesus could respond to all who came to him.

4. We need to recognize that we might not like or immediately understand what we are told. Even Jesus had those who came to him who did not react positively to his answers to their questions.

Books and Places

A final category of "friends" that has often proven helpful to many of us is not from the living persons category at all. Instead, these guides are the messages and support from God offered to us in some of the books we read or reflected in certain places we visit.

The type of friendship that books can offer us may be more important than we expect. In some cases, depending on our situation, the word of God may even come to us *primarily* through our reading. To avoid such opportunities for grace can sometimes dangerously stunt the maturity of our spiritual life.

I have found that more often than not when people who are in ministry come to me to discuss some stress or anxiety they are experiencing in life, they have all but given up spiritual reading. Yet books could help them break through the type of thinking in which they are trapped. In reality, sacred scripture and other readings, including the spiritual classics, are essential for most of us if we are to maintain a continued sense of perspective and freshness in our attitude toward life.

When we feel lost and spiritually cold, a few good words from a spiritually rich volume can fan the embers of hope in us and offer clarity. Avoiding such a rich source of help doesn't make sense, even if—maybe especially if—we feel "down" or too upset to sit and read. In such instances I suggest the following steps:

1. Do not listen to your negative

thoughts.

2. Sit and quiet yourself by closing your eyes.

3. Recite a short prayer.

4. Open your eyes and read a few lines (perhaps those you have underlined in the past) from a favorite book.

5. Ponder the words slowly and with gentle respect.

The results of this exercise are usually positive.

Although we don't hear much about it today, the places we visit and those in which we live and work are also important to the development of our spiritual life. It need not be a famous place of pilgrimage; it could be merely a rock by the ocean or a street in our hometown. But there are places in our lives that remind us of the Lord and in which we seem to breathe more easily and understand God's wishes for us more clearly. Not to heighten our awareness of such places and to avoid visiting them personally or through imagery, seems foolish. For example, a particular hospital chapel in New York City and a certain small lake surrounded by mountains in

Newfoundland were, and still are, special places of peace for me. When feeling un-centered in prayer, I often recall them in my mind's eye, and the images help me settle down.

I also find that visiting places where others have experienced significant encounters with God is good for me as well. When I come to lead a retreat or workshop for a community of persons in ministry, I usually spend some time in their chapel, a place that has been the setting over the years of great prayers and tears of joy, sadness, anguish, and hope. These places have a special history of encounter with God in which we can participate if only we have the desire and take the time to do so.

Many of the ordinary places we go every day can be wonderful settings in which to meet God, but we need to be open to the Lord's surprising presence in them. Too often we are caught up in a special place where we will be in the future (for example, a retreat house), and as a result we are not sensitive to God in the ordinary. Thus we waste the grace available to us here and now. We need the intention and the willingness to expend the little bit of energy necessary to avail ourselves of this gift.

We can only appreciate ourselves as God intended us to be when we begin to value the gift of ordinariness. The beauty of ordinariness is especially revealed, supported, and enhanced by the presence of good friends. The prophet, cheerleader, harasser, and an array of spiritual guides make up an interpersonal web that embraces, challenges, and directs us in our journey toward God, especially during difficult times for ourselves and those whom we love.

The following Vietnamese folk tale sums up the import and tone of this chapter:

> In hell, people have chopsticks a yard long so they cannot reach their mouths and so forever suffer a hunger that will never be quieted. In heaven, even though the chopsticks are the same length, everyone is always well fed. The reason for this is simple: In heaven, the people feed one another.

This is, indeed, the real lesson each of us must appreciate about the value of true friendship, and the one to recall every day as we continue on our search to discover God anew within ourselves and in the people around us.

Jesus, Our Spiritual Director

*H*aving looked at the many ways Jesus' friend-ship guided Peter throughout the gospels, let us reflect on this last recorded encounter between them:

Jesus said to Simon Peter a third time, "Simon, son of John, do you love me? Peter felt hurt because he said to him the third time, "Do you love me?" And he said to him, "Lord, you know everything; you know that I love you." Jesus said to him, "Feed my sheep. Very truly, I tell you, when you were younger, you used to fasten your own belt and go wherever you wished. But when you grow old, you will stretch out your hands, and someone else will fasten a belt around you and take you where you do not wish to go. . . ." After this he said to him, "Follow me" (Jn 21:17-19).

Like all good spiritual directors, Jesus asks probing questions, and he repeats them until they bring about the necessary change of heart. By repeating the question three times, Peter is able to recall the pain of his own triple denial of Jesus but also the Lord's healing forgiveness.

Another way Jesus serves as a good director to Peter is by reminding him of the deepest call of his ministry. "Feed my sheep," Jesus says, leading Peter to look beyond his failure to the mission. Following Jesus is never just a matter of interior conversion, it always involves caring for others.

And finally, Jesus shares his own personally learned wisdom with Peter. Just as Jesus suffered, Peter is reminded that he too will suffer in fulfilling his call. Having argued repeatedly with Jesus over his impending cross, Peter now accepts that he too will be led where he would rather not go. Jesus' final words to Peter echo his first words. Jesus says, "Follow me."

- ◆ In silence before the risen Lord, allow him to ask you whatever question he may wish. Offer your response.

Recognizing the Spiritual Directors in Our Lives

◆ Do you have a spiritual director? If so, how has God worked in your life through that person? Give thanks and pray for your director.

◆ If you do not have a director, do you feel the need for one? If so, how would you go about looking for one?

◆ If you do not feel the need for a director, or you haven't been able to find one, how do you experience the guidance of the Spirit in your life?

Finding Your Spiritual Amma or Abba

◆ Have you ever sought out a revered wisdom figure for guidance on a particular issue of importance? Reflect on both the positive and negative dimensions of this experience.

◆ If you could speak to anyone about your spiritual life, who would it be and what would you say?

Meeting God in Books and Places

◆ What spiritual growth reading material has helped you most? Why?

◆ Where are the holy places in your life today? How do you enter them with awareness?

Journal Exercise

◆ Take the role of Peter. Continue the dialogue begun with Jesus in the passage from John 21.

◆ If you are looking for a spiritual director, formulate a written plan to find one.

◆ Write about the qualities of a particular wisdom figure who attracts you.

◆ Make a list of spiritual reading materials that have been important to you and note something significant about each one.

◆ List the places that comprise your "spiritual geography." What is significant about each?

Conclusion

---

*P*eig Sanders lives on the Blasket Islands off the rugged west coast of Ireland. From there, where few trees break the force of the harsh North Atlantic winds, she offers this wise comment on friendship: "It is in the shelter of each other that people live." If we want to live deeply spiritual lives ourselves, and help others do likewise, it can be no other way.

It takes energy to be a sensitive friend; and it takes understanding and love. By reflecting on our friendships, as we have tried to do in this book, we learn how to nurture the particular gifts we have and grow in our openness toward others.

Friendship also requires humility. Humility is the ability to be truthful and realistic about who we are and what we have to give. Humility leads us to be grateful for the gift of friendship that we have received, and also to acknowledge that we still have far to go. It leads us to pray each day for patience, wisdom, and forgiveness. Without such attitudes, we will be quickly disillusioned by the trials that friendship brings.

But more than trials, friendship brings joy. It offers us shelter from the storms of life, a safe harbor where in the security of knowing we are loved and accepted as we are, we can pause and reflect. There we hear the words that we most need and long for. There we receive the honest challenge of the prophet, the gentle encouragement of the cheerleader, or the impish nudge of the harasser. There we find the wise guidance of a true soul-friend.

In an honest friendship we not only learn about ourselves, we encounter God. In the midst of our ordinariness, we discover God's presence in ourselves, in the other, and in the relationship we share.

References

Downey, Michael. *The New Dictionary of Catholic Spirituality* (Collegeville, MN: Liturgical Press, 1993).

Gratton, Carolyn. *The Art of Spiritual Guidance* (New York: Crossroad, 1992).

Guenther, Margaret. *Holy Listening: The Art of Spiritual Direction* (Boston, MA: Cowley Publications, 1992).

Heschel, Abraham Joshua. *The Insecurity of Freedom* (Philadelphia, PA: The Jewish Publication Society of America, 1966).

Hinnebusch, Paul. *Friendship in the Lord* (Notre Dame, IN: Ave Maria Press, 1974).

John of the Cross. Quoted in Thomas Dubay *Seeking Spiritual Direction* (Ann Arbor, MI: Servant Publications, 1993).

Jones, Alan. *Exploring Spiritual Direction* (New York: Seabury, 1982).

Jones, Timothy K. *Mentor and Friend: Building Friendships that Point to God* (Batavia, IL: Lion Publishing, 1991).

Mooney, Philip. *Belonging Always: Reflections on Uniqueness* (Chicago: Loyola University Press, 1987).

McKenzie, John L. *Dictionary of the Bible* (Milwaukee, WI: The Bruce Publishing Co., 1965).

Nomura, Yoshi. *Desert Wisdom* (New York: Doubleday, 1982).

Nouwen, Henri J. M. *Making All Things New* (San Francisco, CA: Harper & Row, 1981).

St. Exupery, Antoine. *The Little Prince* (New York: Harcourt Brace, 1943).

Sellner, Edward C. *Mentoring: The Ministry of Spiritual Kinship* (Notre Dame, IN: Ave Maria Press, 1990).

Wicks, Robert J. *Seeking Perspective* (Mahwah, NJ: Paulist Press, 1991).

Wicks, Robert J. *Touching the Holy: Ordinariness, Self-Esteem and Friendship* (Notre Dame, IN: Ave Maria Press, 1992).

Dr. Robert J. Wicks is Professor and Director of Program Development for the Graduate Programs in Pastoral Counseling at Loyola College in Maryland. Dr. Wicks, who received his doctorate in psychology from Hahnemann Medical College, also has taught in universities and professional schools of psychology, medicine, social work, theology, and nursing.

In addition to his faculty position and clinical work, Dr. Wicks is general editor of *Illumination Books*, a book review editor, and a member of the editorial board of *Human Development*. Dr. Wicks has also published several audiotape presentations and over thirty books, including the *Handbook of Spirituality for Ministers;* the two-volume *Clinical Handbook of Pastoral Counseling;* and *After Fifty* (all from Paulist Press), and *Touching the Holy* and *Seeds of Sensitivity*, both published by Ave Maria Press. He lives in Ellicott City, Maryland with his wife Michaele who teaches theology. They have one daughter, Michaele Aileen.

Robert M. Hamma is editorial director at Ave Maria Press, where he also directs Spiritual Book Associates book club. He holds an M.A. in theology from the University of Notre Dame as well as an M.Div. degree. He is the author of *Let's Say Grace: Mealtime Prayers for Family Occasions Throughout the Year;* and *Together at Baptism,* a commentary on the Rite of Baptism for parents and godparents. He is the author of *Along Your Desert Journey* and the editor of *A Catechumen's Lectionary* (Paulist Press), a widely-used resource for the R.C.I.A. He and his wife, Kathryn, have three children—Peter, Christine, and Sarah—and have co-authored several *Catholic Updates* about celebrating feasts and seasons of the liturgical year at home.